BOOK TITLE

BINARY MASTERY LAB

By Vincent Kirui

CONTENTS

Contents

This is a convenient XML table in which each step is scheduled by day, including stakes, daily profit goals, and

ABOUT THIS BOOK

Greetings from the Binary Mastery Lab! If you're reading this, you got the Premium Binary Profit Lab bot for Binary.com and Deriv. This is the special version from BPL, which is part of our trading strategy: binary bot trading with minimal losses with full retraining and training in the correct use of bots

Our team can proudly state that in this book you will be able to get the fullest possible amount of knowledge on how to use binary bots with maximum efficiency. This information is relevant and has no analogs in the field of Binary/derivative bots.

We will present a pre-training analysis as well as visual graphs on how to determine the best moments for auto trading. Do not be in a hurry to be scared, we have published this book in the maximum accessible presentation, and after studying it, you will understand that profitable trading bots are not difficult.

You will also be able to use some of the information from this book to improve trading with your favorite bots

How does the selection of a bot for Binary/Deriv trading usually happen?

A trader is looking for a bot that will work stably and make a profit all day 24 hours 7 days a week and start testing it for a long r

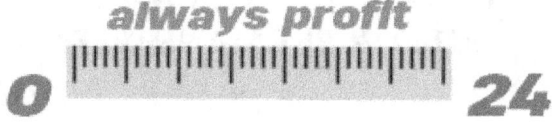

un all
day:

The trader begins to think that if he finds such a bot, he will be able to launch it at any time of the day (highlighted in red in the picture) and always get a profit:

BUT LET'S FACE IT

**IF THERE WAS AT LEAST 1 SUCH
BOT AND IT WAS CONSTANTLY
USED BY AT LEAST 2-5 TRADERS:**

1. **THE BROKER WOULD HAVE GONE
   BANKRUPT LONG AGO AND
   WOULD HAVE CLOSED TRADING
   ON ITS PLATFORM**

2. **AFTER 3-7 DAYS OF TRADING,
   SUCH TRADERS WOULD BE
   BANNED FOR PERMANENTLY**

In our videos, we trade on a confirmed 100% Real Account (Real ID-References) with a short trade of 10 trades, but if you run the bot separately, you are unlikely to see a series of 9-10 wins in a row after a long run.

We use our knowledge and skills for trading, and therefore we draw your attention to the study of this book.

And so before further training, you need to choose one of three ways now*

Standard Version

Standard Version **Standard Version +**

BPL STRATEGY FULL

AUTOMATIC FULL AUTOMATIC

learning our method and improving trading accuracy

0.35$ start stake

0.35$ start stake   2-5 stakes without martingale

40$ daily profit   20$ daily profit

150$ balance required

80$ balance required   50$ balance recommended

Long run the acceptable Long run acceptable version for lower balance**

Most likely you will choose 1 or 2 methods and we understand this, but we also hope that you will be interested in how to get the most out of this bot with the best results and minimal losses with our guide.

We recommend that you remember these 3 ways, you will still need them to study the book

- *We need to understand that trading on synthetic indices (artificial broker markets) we need $ 50- $ 150 to survive. The profit may vary depending on market conditions*

- *All versions are attached to the package*
- *You can start with this version if you are not sure that you can use our strategy*

PREPARING BEFORE LAUNCHING THE BOT

IF YOU CHOOSE THE THIRD WAY, BPL RECOMMENDS USING ALL OF THESE RECOMMENDATIONS, WE ALSO USE ALL OF THEM TOGETHER BEFORE STARTING TRADING USING THE BOT.

Preparation for trading consists of 4 parts
- Technical

- Analytical (simple level)

- Time Planning

- Adjusting Settings

Let's start by saying, that Binary.com and Deriv brokers suggest us different trade types for trading with binary bots (especially for Volatility "synthetic" indices)

We can separate these trade types into 2 groups:

COMPLEX TRADE TYPES	SIMPLE TRADE TYPES
They are directly dependent on the quality of your strategy and can be analyzed using technical indicators and tick analysis:	They are DON'T directly dependent on the quality of your strategy and CAN'T be analyzed using technical indicators and tick analysis:
 - RISE/FALL - HIGHER/LOWER - TOUCH/NO TOUCH - ENDS BETWEEN/ENDS OUTSIDE - STAYS BETWEEN/STAYS OUTSIDE - RESET CALL/RESET PUT	 - ASIANS - DIGIT MATCHES/DIGIT DIFFERS - EVEN/ODD - OVER/UNDER - HIGH/LOW TICKS - ONLY UPS/ONLY DOWNS

Binary bots based on SIMPLE TRADE TYPES work without any logic and strategy, this is a

RANDOM bot, which is why they don't have a direct dependence on a "best trading time"

It has only one way to make a profit with binary bots XML at binary.com platform:

TRADE WITH COMPLEX TRADE TYPES BINARY BOTS

They are directly dependent on the quality of your strategy and can be analyzed using technical indicators and tick analysis.

All strategy and technical indicators work with these fundamental meanings:

- Price movement
- Breakout of consolidation
- Trend following and trend reversals
- Range breakouts
- Price jumps

VPN

<u>You can use VPN services for additional security and protect yourself from binary manipulations.</u> But not everything is so simple

At first thought, you might think that yes, it would be a good idea to use one to trade online, no matter the market or type of trading. They will protect your connection, they will prevent hacks or leaks of personal information and they will help you avoid geo-restrictions. The caveat is that all this protection comes at a price. That price turns out to be the performance of your machine. Using a VPN can cause slow load times and lags that ordinarily would not be a problem but in the fast-paced world of online trading will mean the difference between effective trading and throwing your money away.

If you manage to find a VPN that has minimal impact on your connection speed, then it might be a good idea to use it to

Technical prepearing improve your security but remember, lags will be present nonetheless. To counter this if you are trading BO, our best advice is to stay away from short-term expiry like 60 or 120 seconds and use at least, and I mean at least 15 minute or more likely 30 minute expiry. And considering that scalping needs to be lightning-fast and very accurate, the slightest delay can make the difference between profit and loss.

For the stable operation of the bot and the best trading results to avoid delays, we need high Internet speed

Due to the low speed, the bot may be late with the analysis/opening positions and the bot will enter into unprofitable transactions

Free VPNs will not be able to give us the necessary quality and speed, and sometimes they can even reduce the speed of your Internet.

Therefore, in this guide, we will tell you how to use a paid VPN with the best speed, but always for free!

We recommend to use "WINDSCRIBE" – VPN browser add-on https://windscribe.com/dow nload

After downloading the VPN add-on "Windscribe" you need to set it up correctly:

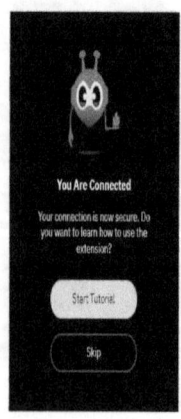 

Select country IP here:

Technical prepearing   Press "Skip recommended: Spain, Portugal, Brazil, Russia, Vietnam, Indonesia, Thailand

You will be given 2 gigabytes of traffic in the free version with high speed, this is quite enough.

But when the limit runs out, just remove this add-on from your browser and install it again.

<u>Your limit will be 2 gigabytes again and the speed is the same high!</u>

The VPN creates a digital tunnel through which your devices connect to the internet and Binary.com/Deriv websites without anyone else knowing about it. The IP address is the main marker that the broker uses to identify you on its platform. To avoid any manipulation on the part of the broker, we recommend changing the IP address every 2-3 days

Incognito Browser Mode

Most traders have tried incognito mode (aka private browsing) on their trading computer at some time, it makes you feel protected

What is Incognito Mode or Private Browsing?
The terms "incognito mode" and "private browsing" are different names for the same feature. For example, when you use this feature, Google Chrome or Opera opens an

Technical prepearing Incognito Window. But Firefox and Apple Safari will open a Private Window.

Regardless of what you call it, these features work pretty much the same way in any browser.

When you are roaming the Binary.com or Deriv broker's web pages in normal mode, the browser saves your browsing history and session information. It shares this information with their sites.

Brokers have long learned how to extract this information for their benefit, up to interference in the work of bots

That's why we recommend Incognito, in incognito or private mode, web browsers follow enhanced privacy rules. Specifically, they don't save your browsing history, cookies, or site data. So there is less information available for a website to extract from the browser.

Alternatively, you could delete your history and cookies at the end of each browsing session. This will achieve the same result. But incognito mode is a fast workaround to avoid saving this information in the first place.

Instead, you can use incognito mode to log in to multiple accounts. Even though a private window creates cookies just like a regular window, those cookies are restricted to the private session.

So, you can use incognito mode to log into more than one account at the same time.

This can be especially handy when you want to duplicate binary bots trading from one account to the other.

When you use incognito mode on your trading computer, the browser doesn't save your session data. But your IP address is still visible to websites you visit, that's why this combination of VPN + Incognito Mode is also recommended.

Technical prepearing

Technical prepearing **CCleaner & software**

The methods listed above are necessary for us for personal protection from the broker, but we also need to prepare a computer and be sure of the speed, since seconds can decide everything on tick trading

Let's start with the main thing:

WE STRONGLY RECOMMEND TO CLEAR YOUR COOKIE, HISTORY, CACHE in your browser before trading with binary bots in https://bot.binary.com/bot.html and https://app.deriv.com/bot

Are you subscribing to a binary broker and starting to trade without deleting cookies? Careful, because you're throwing money away.

A cookie is similar to a small text file that is released without your knowledge on your computer by the website you've visited. It's useful to save your preferences

Technical prepearing and improve the site's performance in the foreseeable case of your subsequent visit.

Cookies are not harmful in themselves, but as a broker uses them to keep track of your visit, especially if earlier, you probably do not want this to be recorded.

This aspect, which seems unimportant, actually has great economic value, and disregarding it means that you are throwing money right out the window!

The broker, or any broker as you know, is always looking for new investors/traders to increase the odds of their profits, and spend considerable resources on advertising and economic agreements with sites that help you in this purpose. When you open an account with a new broker, probably after clicking on a banner ad, or a text containing a link, they will provide "rewards" to the affiliated site you came from. Logically this does not result in anything on your part, apart from some pretty incentives, which are mostly not acceptable to all traders, and should they profit, they would temporarily prohibit making withdrawals.

As you know and have noticed more than once, a broker always gives more chances to win for new traders (you might also notice that new bots trade well, but their performance deteriorates over time)

And when you delete cookies and cache before trading, you force the broker to use its algorithms against itself. In theory, this method can increase your chance to profit by 10-15%

Tips to great PC performance for Binary.com and Deriv auto-trading:

- Download Piriform CCleaner
  https://www.piriform.com/ccleaner
- Run this at the end of the day every day. Also, make sure you have it updated weekly
- Download Malwarebytes
  https://www.malwarebytes.org/mwb
  -download/

Technical prepearing - Run full scan every 2 days
– Also make sure you have it
updated weekly
- Download Clean up under primary
download site –
http://www.stevengould.org/index.p
hp?option=com_content&task=view
&id=29&Itemid=223

CCleaner is a mandatory program, and
Malwarebytes and CleanUP are optional,
their presence is not necessary

Time Synchronization

By our strategy, binary bot trading takes
place at the recommended time.

We will tell you about the recommended
time later in this book (see "applied" part).
But for the time to work correctly, we need

to synchronize. And this is already part of the technical training

To do this, we need the Atomic program (you can find it in the bot package)

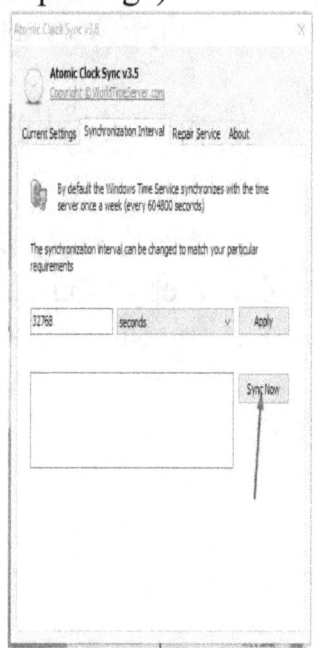

This is the general summary of technical preparation before starting a binary bot:

1. VPN
2. INCOGNITO BROWSER MODE

3. CCLEANER
4. TIME SYNCHRONIZATION BY
     ATOMIC.EXE

Additional recommendations that can
improve technical preparing

5. Also don't use EDGE (Internet
    Explorer). Use the latest version
    of Google Chrome 6. Also never
    use WI-FI unless you have a
    gaming router. Use Ethernet
    Ethernet-connected PC.
7. Never trade in two browser tabs in
    parallel (in one browser)
8. Use only a computer or laptop to
    trade. Do not trade on the phone
9. PC and browser must always be
    active, not sleep or off

Analytical prepearing   HOW EASY USE CHART WITHOUT ANALYZE
FOR FIND BEST PERIOD TO TRADE WITH BOT

We have smoothly
moved on to the
second stage on
the correct use of
the bot This is the
second on the list
but the first in the
importance section
on preparation

Many fans have often asked us about how
we use the chart to trade with this bot and
finally, we are ready to explain our secrets
on the chart that you can also use

**Let's agree right away, yes, this section
of preparation requires the use of a
graph, <u>but you do not have to analyze
anything and do not have knowledge of
graph analysis</u>**

We recommend checking the market
before starting any bot playing in a good
market will optimize the winning chance
and minimize the risk, especially if we use
martingale. Based on our deep testing,

Technical prepearing there are 2 simple alternatives to find the right moment:

1. Smart Trader Chart in binary.com

3 things must be considered: Space, Range, and Tick Movement. Good markets are usually formed if they all meet the criteria:

a) Space (look at the picture below)

Volatility 50: at least 0.1000 points
Volatility 75: at least 100.0000 points
Vovolatility 100: at least 2.00 points

b) Range (look at the picture below) It's good to play in at least 6 spaces. So, get ready when the chart shows the transition from 5 to 6 spaces to take momentum.

c) Tick Movement (look at the picture below) Tick chart must show a strong trend and clear direction, and the point between ticks must be relatively small (there is no jumping / sudden point

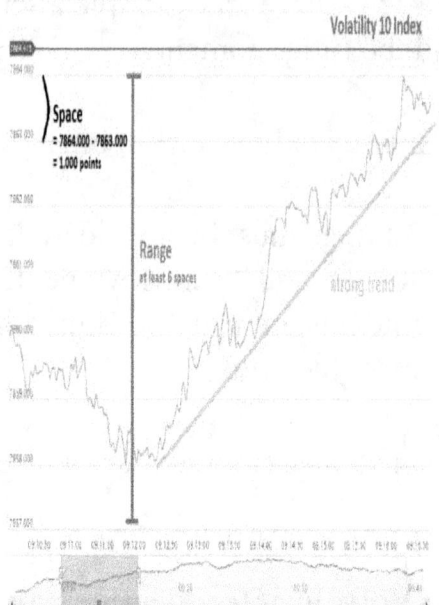

Avoid tick patterns shown in the picture below. Even though the range has met the criteria (6 spaces), the space is less than 1.000 points (for Volatility 10) & ticks do random movement with a lot of jumping points.

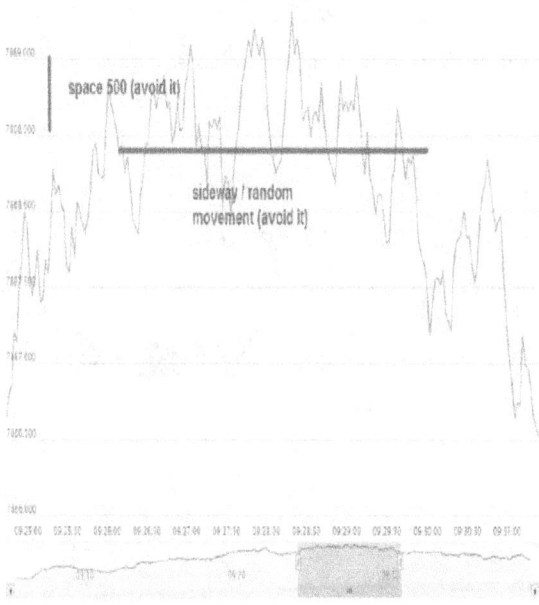

Running if market conditions look like the picture below
R
U
N
Examples of characteristic ticks that form candles like this,

When tik at the end of the candle, e.g.: the top edge of the candle before moving to the next candle, tic down the length quarter candle
If the candle characteristics on average like this continue running Bot,

Be careful or can be stopped immediately if the market conditions show like the picture below
if the tail of the candle decreases and the candle becomes longer there will usually be a trend, or the market moves sharper, thus making a long gap when Bot opens position when conditions like this you can stop Bot.

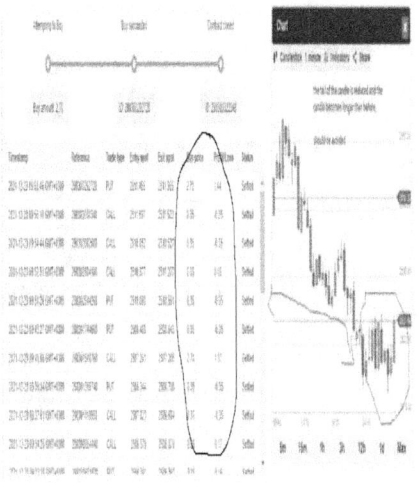

Easy way to find market sideway

Use the EMA line
Market Sideway when EMA
Lines are in the middle

Hopefully, the above
tips can make your trading better

Market selection

How easy is it to find a suitable Volatility Index?

At the broker Binary.com/Deriv There are 12 synthetic volatility indices.
Volatility Index: 10 – 100; Bear / Bull Markets
Before starting the bot, we need to determine which index is best to choose.
It is easy to do this with candles, without resorting to serious knowledge of analysis

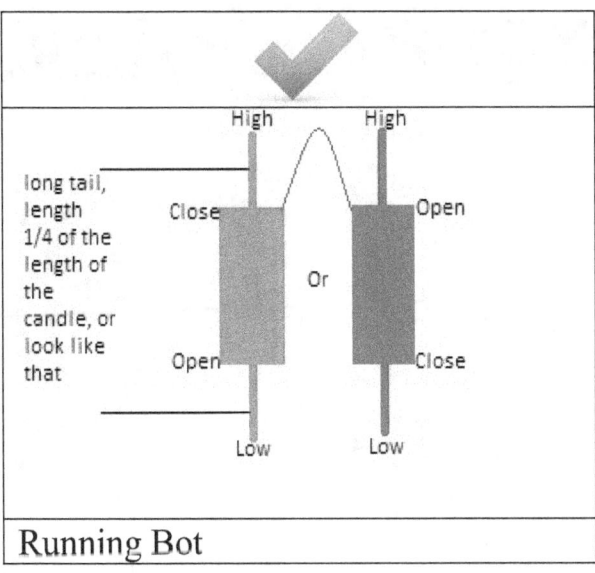

Running Bot

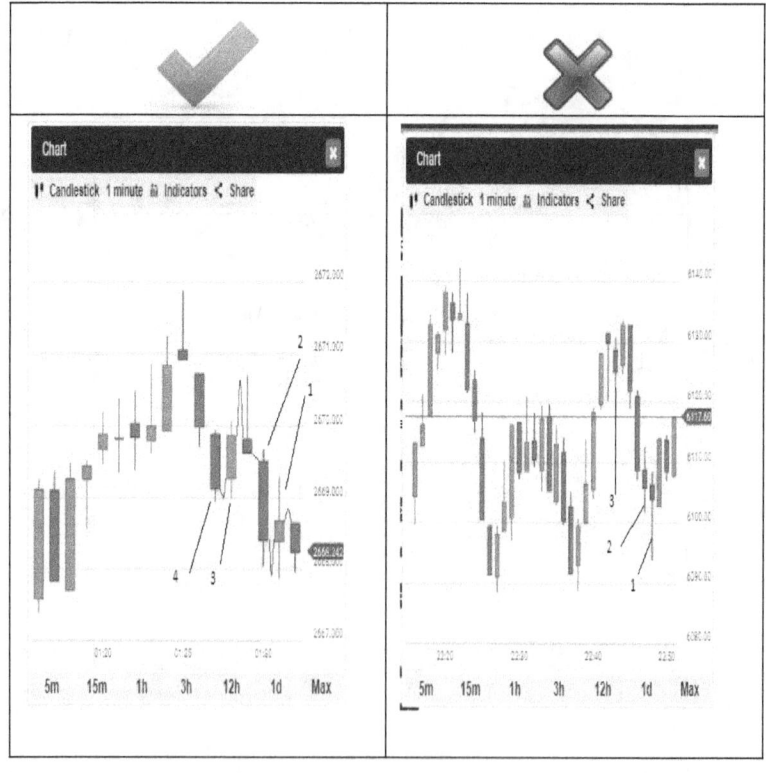

More candle with tail	Less candle with tail
continue running Bot	Stop Bot or choose another Market

Signals to avoid Auto-Trading with Bot

Please Note:

Even though we have entered a good market, it will not guarantee we always win, anything can still happen, but statistically, it has better & safer results.

Before playing, load the chart first, this will help to avoid controversial situations related to broker manipulations

BINARY.COM /DERIVE PROVIDES A GREAT OPPORTUNITY FOR LEARNING AND TRAINING TRADE IN VIRTUAL ACCOUNT FIRST PRACTICE

Time planning   CHECK STATUS BEFORE PLAY

https:// binaryc om.stat uspage. io/

Few traders know,

but we also advise you to use this site in
To avoid money losses
For technical reasons when you trade on a
real account

If you see red or
yellow sections in
the last 1-3 hours,
then wait a little
and then start
trading

Time planning
THE BEST TIME TO RUN

All strategy and technical indicators work
with these fundamental meanings:

- Price movement
- Breakout of consolidation
- Trend following and trend reversals
- Range breakouts
- Price jumps

Consequently, if you know the best time of price movement or breakout of consolidation it can increase your profit chance to 50% and you will have the advantage over traders, who don't use the best time for trading.

Technically, Volatility indexes price forms support and resistance on each time frame. The best time to trade Volatility indexes is when the price reacts to previous support or resistance levels.

Reactions such as the formation of 1. Trend continuation, 2. Price reversal or 3. Retesting and bouncing off on support and resistance levels are also important.

Fundamentally, Volatility indexes do not react to news. However, the Volatility index price positively correlates with the USD Index (DXY) and some USD-based Forex pairs such as USDJPY. XAUUSD or Gold negatively correlates with Volatility indexes some of the time.

Consequently, the time of price movement or breakout of consolidation occurs around the following time;

03:00 GMT

07:00 GMT

11:00 GMT

15:00 GMT

19:00 GMT

23:00 GMT

The most important time is the 8:00 GMT and 16:30 GMT. (LONDON TRADING SESSION)

Results from our research on the best time to trade **Volatility indexes indicate** that major trend reversals, range breakouts, and price jumps happen around 8:00 GMT and 16:30 GMT.

MARKET TIMING FOR DIFFERENT TIME ZONES:

- Pacific (00:00 — 8:30 GMT)
- Asian (13:00 — 21:30 GMT)
- European (9:00 — 17:30 GMT)
- American (04:00 — 12:30 GMT)

Never let the bot run without stopping or with a higher target. If you run bots all day, then you will lose money. Don't use the bot on the 'bad' hours, or it will ruin swallow your money.

We can't rule out the fact that there may be an occasional range or consolidating price movement at a particular time, but this happens once in a while.

Traders with sniper skills usually take trade positions with Binary Bot around 8:00 and 16:30 GMT.

Please Note: Do not forget to synchronize time using the Atomic.exe program, which we described in the chapter
"technical preparing"

Time Planing   BEST TRADING TIME (DAYS)

We did our research about the best days for trading.
We involve our big testing group with 40 customers and 2 months of daily tests.

In this research, we determine that MONEY ($) LOSS RISK is very low from MONDAY to FRIDAY (~5-12%) and very high at weekends SATURDAY-SUNDAY (~30-40%)

If you trade over a weekend or holiday you're going to be faced with slippage and unpredictability when the market comes back into session. Great way to lose money! This is a bad time to trade.

WE STRONGLY DON'T RECOMMEND TRADING ON WEEKEND DAYS SATURDAY, SUNDAY

SECRET INFORMATION:

We strongly don't recommend trading with every binary bot (incl. Venema PRO v3) in Volatility Indexes on these days: 1, 8, 10 calendar dates of each every month

We keep in secret resource of this information, but our testing research confirm this fact after bad results in every month with this dates.

Sunday	Monday	Tuesday	Wednesday	Thursday	Friday	Saturday
				1	2	3
4	5	6	7	8	9	10
11	12	13	14	15	16	17
18	19	20	21	22	23	24
25	26	27	28	29	30	31

www.a-printable-calendar.com

_Time management and duration of trading sessions

SCALPING / SHORT TRADING

if you chose the 3rd way at the beginning of this book and followed all our instructions you can run this bot 10-15 runs without martingale and 90%-100% accuracy and take profit

LONG RUN

<u>If you chose the 1st way at the beginning of this book,</u> we recommend: 4-8 trade sessions per/day ;

1 trade session = 45-50 minutes
Rest 10-15 minutes with clean cache/cookies in the browser (you can also use CCleaner or incognito mode in

<u>if you chose the 2nd way at the beginning of this book,</u> you can trade with this bot 24 hours in an extreme-long run

Settings AdjustmentVIRTUAL FILTERS (VIRTUAL LOSS/VIRTL

Most of the settings in our bot are ready for trading and do not require changes (you do not need to change the duration of trading), but there are settings that you need to use and there are mandatory and optional

Mandatory to use: Virtual Filters (Virtual Loss / Virtua Win); Barrier Offsets

Optional to use/change: Default Candle Interval; Stakes List

Now let's talk about the required settings and Virtual Filters (Virtual Loss / Virtual Win)

Virtual Loss: This filter means how many consecutive virtual losses the bot will wait in one row before starting trading

For example: if "Virtual Loss" is set to "3" – the bot will wait for 3 consecutive virtual losses in one row and after that bot will open first position and so on.

This is one of the main filters and it helps to avoid losses in real account trading

Virtual Win: This filter means how many consecutive virtual wins the bot will wait in one row before starting trading

For example: if "Virtual Loss" is set to "2" – the bot will wait 3 consecutive virtual wins in one row and after that bot will open the first position and so on.

This filter helps to determine and find win streaks

⚙ It has 3 different presets for Virtual Filters (if you choose 1st and 3rd ways to trade with a bot):

Virtual Manager: 1	Virtual Manager: 1
Virtual Manager: 5	
Virtual Loss: 1	Virtual Loss: 3
Virtual Loss: 4	
Virtual Win: 1	Virtual Win: 1
Virtual Win: 1	

How to determine when to change settings for Virtual Filters:

If you see the yellow notification from the broker about the update

⚠ We're updating our site in a short while. Some services may be temporarily unavailable.

We recommend stopping the bot and using one of these settings presets (which we have listed above and periodically changing them among themselves)

<u>If you chose the 2nd way at the beginning of this book</u>, you can trade with default settings "Virtual Loss" – "1" and "Virtual Win" – "1", it will be enough for the version with safety money-management in a long run

Settings AdjustmentOFFSET BARRIERS. SECRET #1 !

48

OK let's look at the following important parameters that you can choose

Offset Barriers are one of the main settings that are responsible for the profit level during the trading of this bot.

You can find the settings in this block

	set	_Barrier Lounge A ▾	to	165
	set	_Barrier Lounge B ▾	to	175

This unique bot has twin barriers in one bot you need to monitor the correctness of the settings

The bottom line is that if you chose the 3rd way at the beginning of the book and you will trade with our instructions, you need to make sure that the payout for the established barrier is 50% (as in our videos)

Offset barriers can change every day and the percentage of payments on them will shift accordingly!

Before starting the bot in a 3rd way, you
need to check at the main Binary.com /
Deriv site that your current offset barriers
give you 50% profit per/ trade
**https://smarttrader.deriv.com/en/trading
.html**

In the screenshot you may see, that barrier
+153 will give a 50.1% profit payout with
5.01$ profit per 10$ stake.
This is what we need

By analogy, you can also set up payouts for each volatility index.

We will send you the versions of the bot for all indexes with current barriers at the time of writing, but before you start, you will still need to check their payouts on the main site

If at the beginning of the book you chose 1st way (martingale) or 2nd way (safe martingale) then we need payout settings in 40%

AND NOW YOU WILL SEE THE FIRST SECRET OF OFFSET BARRIERS IN THIS BOT CHECK FIRST SCREENSHOT

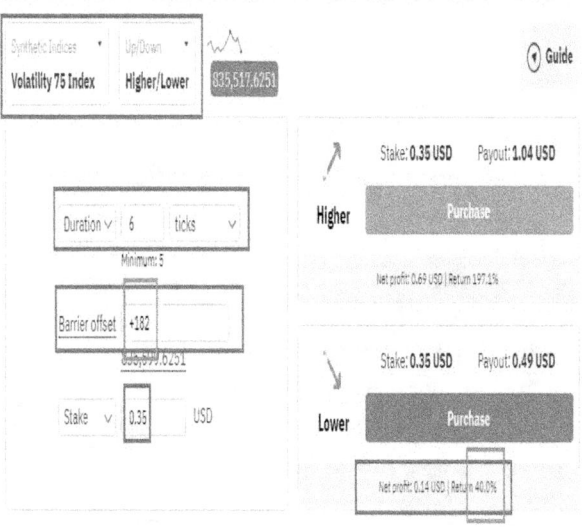

YOU MAY SEE THAT IT NEEDS A
"182" OFFSET BARRIER TO WIN A
40% PROFIT PAYOUT

OK, CHECK THE SECOND
SCREENSHOT

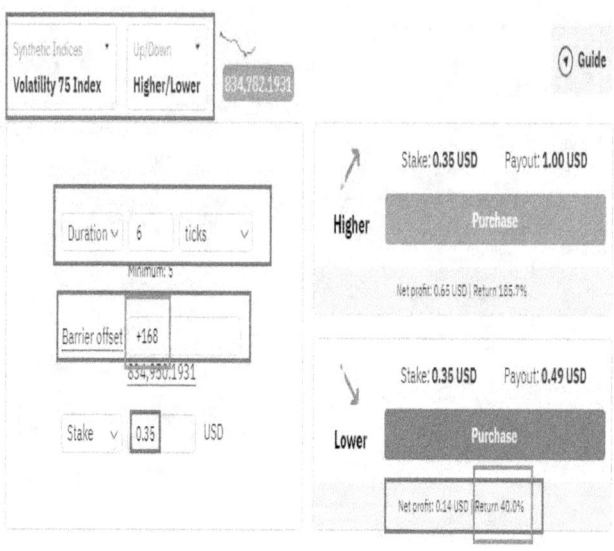

YOU MAY SEE THAT IT NEEDS "168" OFFSET BARRIER TO WIN A 40% PROFIT PAYOUT TOO!

182 AND 168 BARRIER OFFSETS GIVE THE SAME PROFIT AT DIFFERENT BARRIERS!

THE DIFFERENCE BETWEEN 182 AND 168 (14 POINTS!!) IS HUGE WITHIN THE AUTO TRADE!

AND OF COURSE, WE NEED TO TAKE 182 AS A SAFER BARRIER FOR US!

THIS IS THE PURPOSE OF CHECKING
THE BARRIERS ON THE MAIN SITE
BEFORE TURNING ON THE BOT, WE
NEED TO DETERMINE A SAFE
BARRIER FOR A 40% PAYOUT

Settings Adjustment   OFFSET BARRIERS. SECRET #2 !

And so after studying secret #1, we realized
that the percentages of payments on offset
barriers can change daily and we need to
check the barriers on the main site
Binary.com / Deriv

But why are these barriers changing and
what does it depend on?

Offset Barriers directly depend on the
CHART PIPS

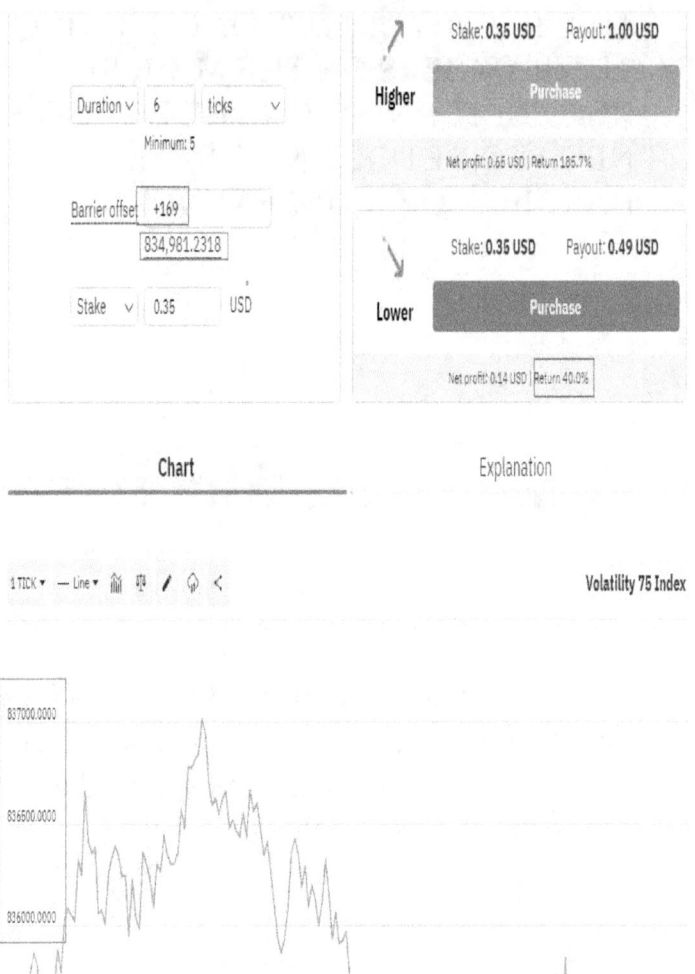

In this screenshot, you may see that if chart pips ~83700 (chart) or 834,981.2318 (tab) barrier 169 will give a profit of 40%

If the chart pips will change in a big way, for example to ~86200 or 861,182.3391

We will need to increase the offset barrier to keep the payout at $40 (from 169 to 191), otherwise, if we keep the old barrier, our payout will decrease to 38%

If the chart pips will change in a downward way, for example to ~79200 or 791,182.3391

We will need to decrease the offset barrier to keep the payout at $40 (from 169 to 153), otherwise, if we keep the old barrier, our payout will increase to 43%

NOW LET'S GO DIRECTLY TO SECRET #2

THE GREATER THE VALUE OF OFFSET BARRIERS, THE MORE TRADE WE WILL WIN (WE WILL HAVE A LARGE MARGIN OF PRICE MOVEMENT IN TRADING HIGHER/LOWER)

THE LOWER THE VALUE OF OFFSET
BARRIERS, THE MORE TRADES WE
WILL LOSE (WE WILL HAVE A
LOWER MARGIN OF PRICE
MOVEMENT IN TRADING
HIGHER/LOWER)

THE CRITICAL VALUE STARTS
AFTER 72000

HOW CAN WE AVOID FREQUENT
LOSSES WHEN LOWERING
BARRIERS?

WE NEED TO COMBINE AUTOMATIC
VIRTUAL FILTERS (VIRTUAL
LOSS/VIRTUAL FILTER) AND OUR
METHOD "PROGRESSIVE SPY TRICK"

"PROGRESSIVE SPY TRICK"

 We also use this trick before run the bot on Real Account in our videos :

1. open 2 different browsers with the virtual and real accounts it's important to run 2 different browsers because it will not work in 1 browser

2. run a virtual account and wait for 2 consecutive losses in one row

3. when 2 virtual losses hit we run the second tab with a real account

4. this method will work together with virtual loss in Venema M-PRO 5 for the best avoiding the losses

You can use this method for your profit trading in a short/scalping for 10-20 runs

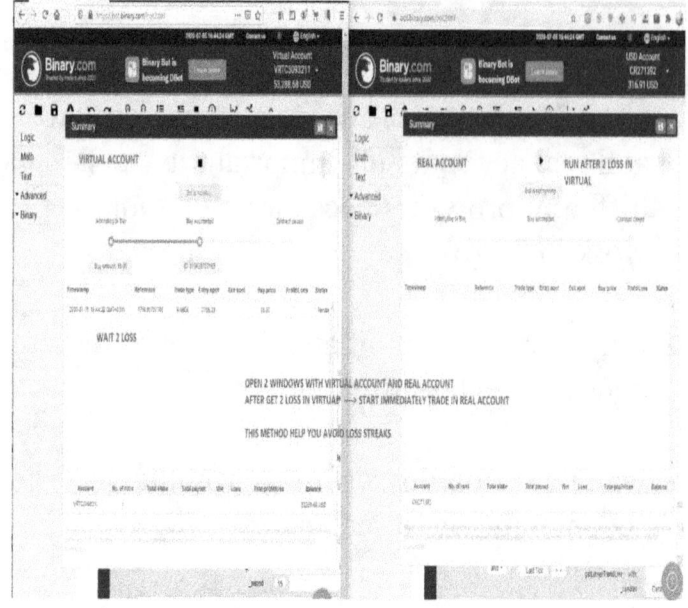

WAIT 2 LOSS

OPEN 2 WINDOWS WITH VIRTUAL ACCOUNT AND REAL ACCOUNT

AFTER GET 2 LOSS IN VIRTUAP ---> START IMMEDIATELY TRADE IN REAL ACCOUNT

THIS METHOD HELP YOU AVOID LOSS STREAKS

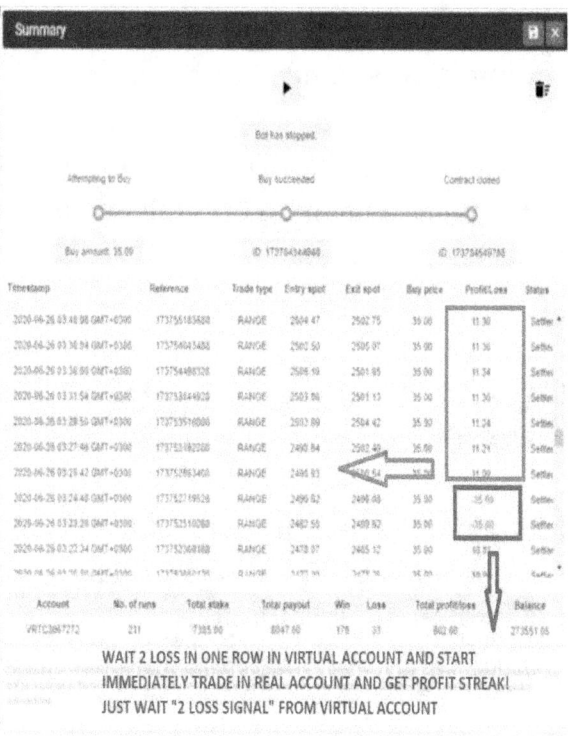

This is the example screenshots with the Premium RANGE bot which we trade with this trick. This trick can work for any binary bot. Use your VIRTUAL account and get maximum from that!

Settings Adjustment   Default Candle Interval

OK, we have sorted out with you the mandatory settings that you need to monitor.

Let's now look at the additional settings that you don't have to change, but you can do it if you want to experiment

One of these settings is the Default Candle Interval

Many traders do not notice this setting or may not know about it, but it also makes sense (according to the situation)

In this screenshot, you can see that the Default Candle Interval is set to "2", i.e. every second candle is filtered and ignored, if we traded the bot on UPTREND on each candle, we would lose, but since every second red candle was ignored, we would trade without losses

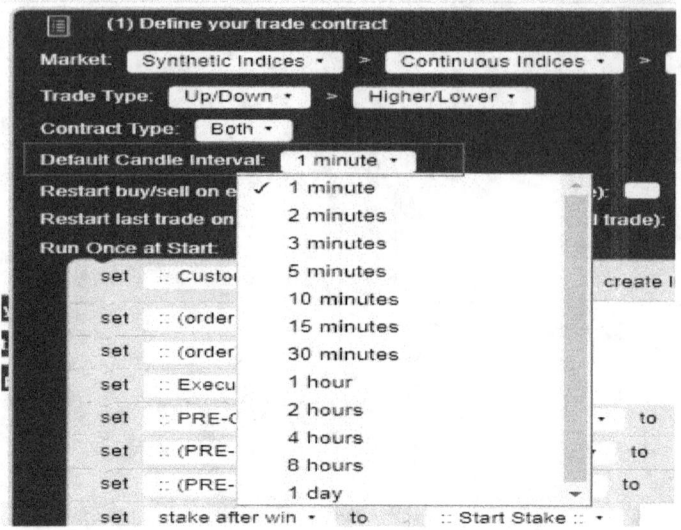

You can set Default Candle
Intervals here:

Please note that the higher the
indicator of Default Candle
Interval is, the more candlesticks
will be filtered and the slower
trades will be opened

If you want, you can experiment
with these settings
 (We can recommend values 1, 2,
5, 15)

Settings Adjustment

Customer's Stake List

In our bot, we have implemented a unique feature for the selection of stakes, you can customize each step of trading for yourself if you use martingale

99.9% of binary bots do not have such a setting, but thanks to this development, we were able to develop a secure martingale for $80 and 24 hours of trading (if you chose the 2nd way at the beginning of the book)

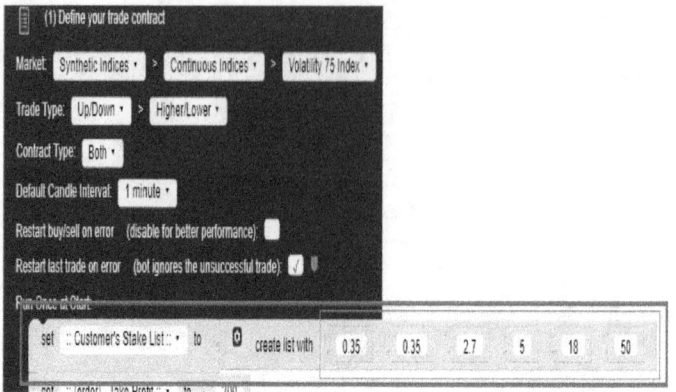

All fields are available for changes and you can adjust the stakes individually.

If you want to trade without martingale, just write in all the fields like this:

"1", "1", "1", "1", "1"

create list with	0.5	0.5	3.8	0.35	0.95	3.8
create list with	0.35	0.95	3.8	13.5	48.6	175.4
create list with	1	2.8	10.4	37.7	135.2	300

We know that among our users there are also traders with large deposits of $ 300- $500 if you have a large deposit and want a turbo profit, you can also try these MM-presets

PROFIT MONEY MANAGEMENT

We recommend you use the "PROFIT PLAN TAB" which you will also find in this package.

This is a convenient XML table in which each step is scheduled by day, including stakes, daily profit goals, and following which you will be able to reach a stable profit

If for any reason this table is not suitable for you, Based on the above, based on the algorithm that the broker uses to withdraw money from traders and if you use our PROGRESSIVE "SPY" TRICK, we recommend setting a take profit of 10$ FOR ONE TRADING SESSION.

After your Take Profit (10$) is reached, stop the bot, and take the rest (15 minutes)

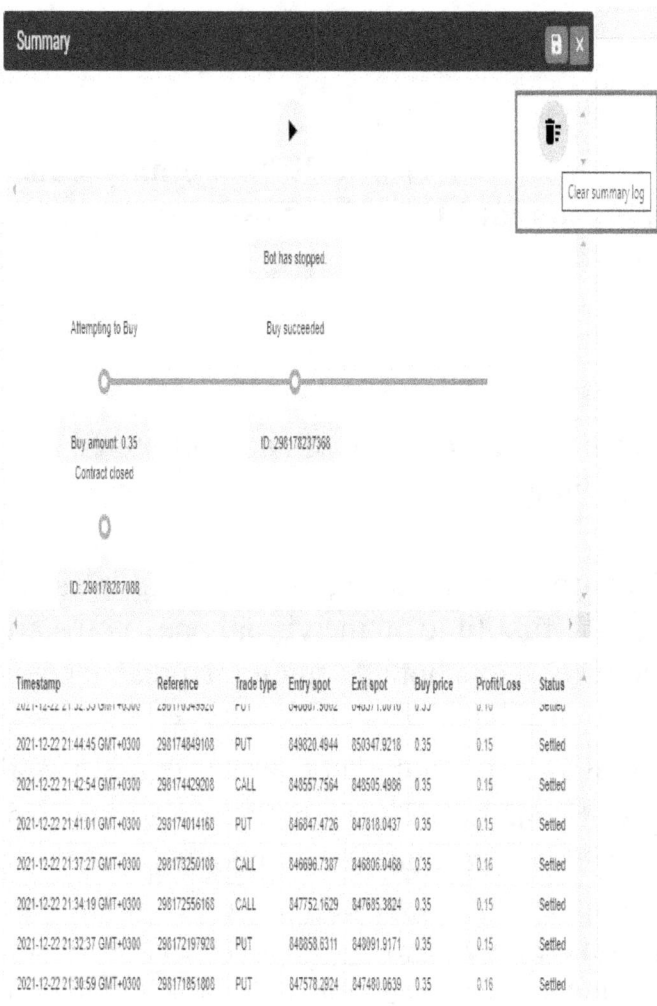

Summary

Bot has stopped.

Attempting to Buy   Buy succeeded

Buy amount: 0.35   ID: 298178237368

Contract closed

ID: 298178287088

Clear summary log

Timestamp	Reference	Trade type	Entry spot	Exit spot	Buy price	Profit/Loss	Status
2021-12-22 21:32:33 GMT+0300	298170345320	PUT	846867.5082	846571.0010	0.35	0.16	Settled
2021-12-22 21:44:45 GMT+0300	298174849108	PUT	849820.4944	850347.9218	0.35	0.15	Settled
2021-12-22 21:42:54 GMT+0300	298174429208	CALL	848557.7564	848505.4986	0.35	0.15	Settled
2021-12-22 21:41:01 GMT+0300	298174014168	PUT	846847.4726	847818.0437	0.35	0.15	Settled
2021-12-22 21:37:27 GMT+0300	298173250108	CALL	846696.7387	846806.0468	0.35	0.16	Settled
2021-12-22 21:34:19 GMT+0300	298172556168	CALL	847752.1629	847685.3824	0.35	0.15	Settled
2021-12-22 21:32:37 GMT+0300	298172197928	PUT	848658.8311	848091.9171	0.35	0.15	Settled
2021-12-22 21:30:59 GMT+0300	298171851808	PUT	847578.2824	847480.0639	0.35	0.16	Settled

Always keep in mind that it is always necessary to clear the trading history between trading sessions, this is very important for success in the next trading sessions!

Why do 99% of binary bots lose your money? How this "loss-algorithm" is work

We bet, that you have often encountered the following situation.

You download the bot, launch it and it trades well for the first time on the virtual one. You start to believe in this bot and run it on a real account.

Many people think that a broker makes them a profit on a virtual account and takes their money from a real account. Many people think that these accounts work differently. But this is the main mistake. It's not about the difference between the virtual and real accounts. If you run them at the same time, you will most likely see trading with the same quotes.

The fact is that the "algorithm for losing your money" works differently.

EXAMPLE:

You have a deposit of 15$
You trade with a RISE/FALL martingale binary bot (random bot from the internet) Your start stake is 1$
You can see 1 consistent loss at the start of the bot after 11 runs

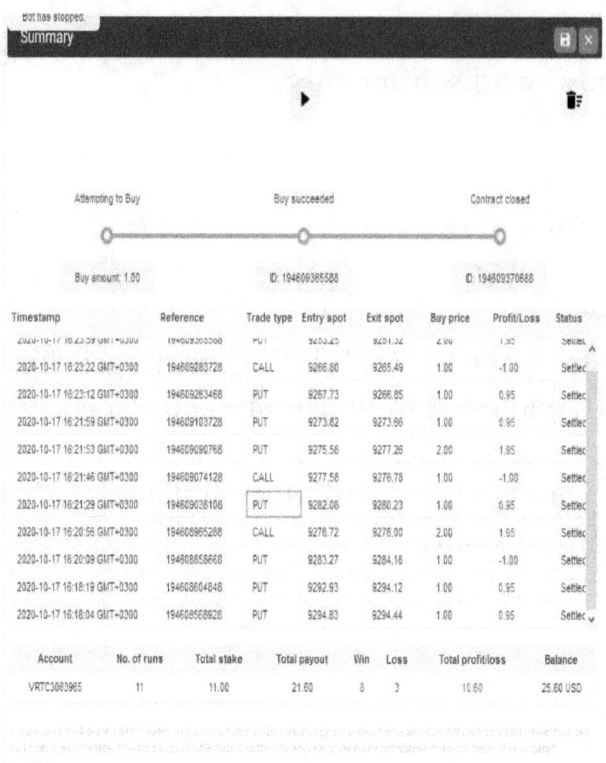

23 runs in total, we met 2 series of 2 consistent losses in one row

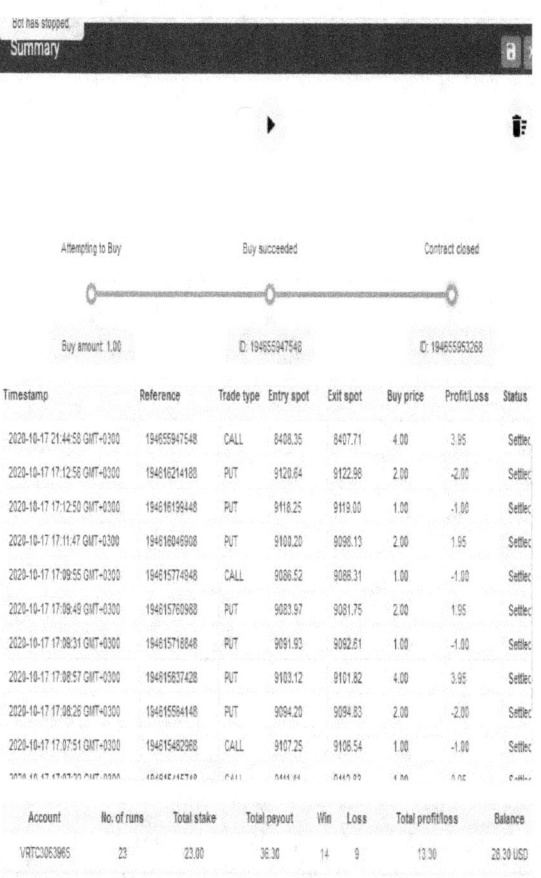

Timestamp	Reference	Trade type	Entry spot	Exit spot	Buy price	Profit/Loss	Status
2020-10-17 21:44:58 GMT+0300	194655947548	CALL	8408.35	8407.71	4.00	3.95	Settled
2020-10-17 17:12:56 GMT+0300	194616214188	PUT	9120.64	9122.98	2.00	-2.00	Settled
2020-10-17 17:12:50 GMT+0300	194616199448	PUT	9118.25	9119.00	1.00	-1.00	Settled
2020-10-17 17:11:47 GMT+0300	194616046908	PUT	9100.20	9098.13	2.00	1.95	Settled
2020-10-17 17:09:55 GMT+0300	194615774948	CALL	9086.52	9088.31	1.00	-1.00	Settled
2020-10-17 17:09:49 GMT+0300	194615760988	PUT	9083.97	9081.75	2.00	1.95	Settled
2020-10-17 17:08:31 GMT+0300	194615718848	PUT	9091.93	9092.51	1.00	-1.00	Settled
2020-10-17 17:08:57 GMT+0300	194615837428	PUT	9103.12	9101.82	4.00	3.95	Settled
2020-10-17 17:08:26 GMT+0300	194615594148	PUT	9094.20	9094.83	2.00	-2.00	Settled
2020-10-17 17:07:51 GMT+0300	194615482968	CALL	9107.25	9106.54	1.00	-1.00	Settled
2020-10-17 17:07:29 GMT+0300	194615457348	CALL	9111.31	9112.93	1.00	0.95	Settled

Account	No. of runs	Total stake	Total payout	Win	Loss	Total profit/loss	Balance
VRTC3063965	23	23.00	36.30	14	9	13.30	26.30 USD

We continued to trade with this random bot until 51 runs, it was a series of 1 and 2 consistent losses until 51 runs, but we started to meet 3 consistent losses in one row after 51 runs

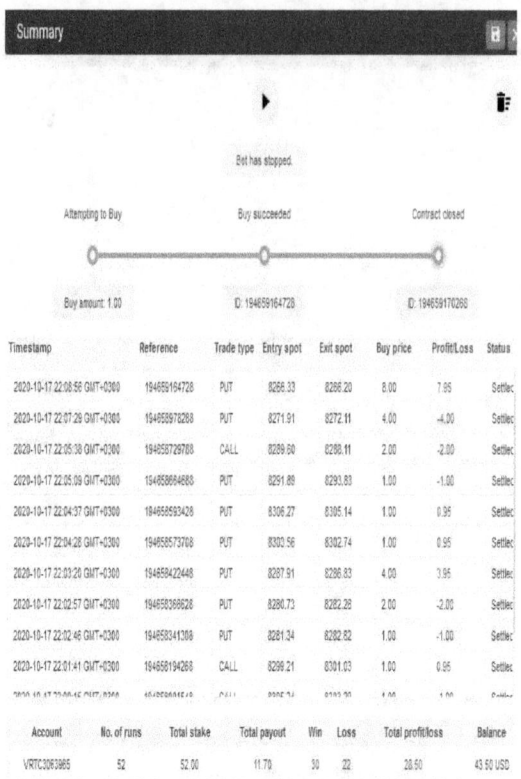

Timestamp	Reference	Trade type	Entry spot	Exit spot	Buy price	Profit/Loss	Status
2020-10-17 22:08:56 GMT+0300	194659164728	PUT	8266.33	8266.20	8.00	7.95	Settled
2020-10-17 22:07:26 GMT+0300	194658976268	PUT	8271.91	8272.11	4.00	-4.00	Settled
2020-10-17 22:05:38 GMT+0300	194658729788	CALL	8289.60	8286.11	2.00	-2.00	Settled
2020-10-17 22:05:09 GMT+0300	194658684688	PUT	8291.89	8293.83	1.00	-1.00	Settled
2020-10-17 22:04:37 GMT+0300	194658593428	PUT	8306.27	8305.14	1.00	0.95	Settled
2020-10-17 22:04:28 GMT+0300	194658573768	PUT	8300.56	8302.74	1.00	0.95	Settled
2020-10-17 22:03:20 GMT+0300	194658422448	PUT	8287.91	8286.83	4.00	3.95	Settled
2020-10-17 22:02:57 GMT+0300	194658368628	PUT	8280.73	8282.28	2.00	-2.00	Settled
2020-10-17 22:02:46 GMT+0300	194658341368	PUT	8281.34	8282.82	1.00	-1.00	Settled
2020-10-17 22:01:41 GMT+0300	194658194268	CALL	8299.21	8301.03	1.00	0.95	Settled
2020-10-17 22:00:45 GMT+0300	194658045648	CALL	8305.74	8303.20	1.00	1.00	Settled

Account	No. of runs	Total stake	Total payout	Win	Loss	Total profit/loss	Balance
VRTC3063965	52	52.00	11.70	30	22	28.50	43.50 USD

We continued to trade with this bot and met 4 consistent losses in one row after 63 runs, The broker started aggressively testing our deposit and started to find our money limit to recover the losses

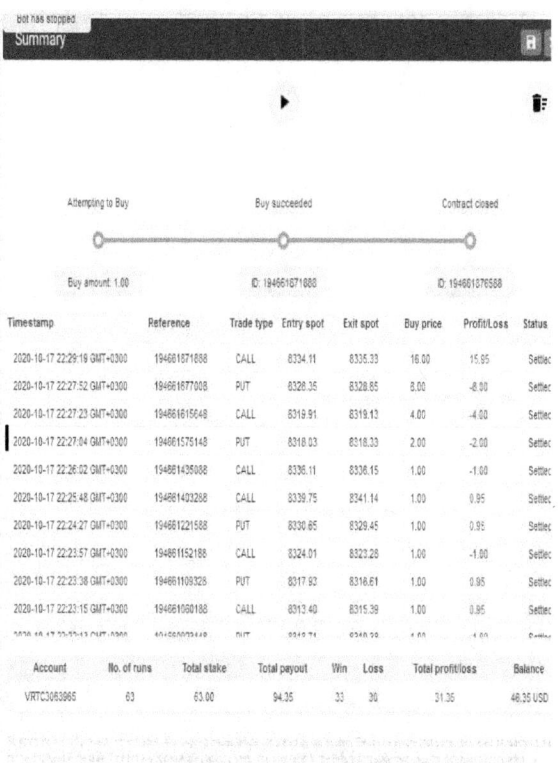

Timestamp	Reference	Trade type	Entry spot	Exit spot	Buy price	Profit/Loss	Status
2020-10-17 22:29:19 GMT+0300	194661871888	CALL	8334.11	8335.33	16.00	15.95	Settled
2020-10-17 22:27:52 GMT+0300	194661677008	PUT	8328.35	8328.85	8.00	-8.00	Settled
2020-10-17 22:27:23 GMT+0300	194661615648	CALL	8319.91	8319.13	4.00	-4.00	Settled
2020-10-17 22:27:04 GMT+0300	194661575148	PUT	8318.03	8318.33	2.00	-2.00	Settled
2020-10-17 22:26:02 GMT+0300	194661435088	CALL	8336.11	8336.15	1.00	-1.00	Settled
2020-10-17 22:25:48 GMT+0300	194661403288	CALL	8339.75	8341.14	1.00	0.95	Settled
2020-10-17 22:24:27 GMT+0300	194661221588	PUT	8330.85	8329.45	1.00	0.95	Settled
2020-10-17 22:23:57 GMT+0300	194661152188	CALL	8324.01	8323.28	1.00	-1.00	Settled
2020-10-17 22:23:38 GMT+0300	194661109328	PUT	8317.93	8318.61	1.00	0.95	Settled
2020-10-17 22:23:15 GMT+0300	194661060188	CALL	8313.40	8315.39	1.00	0.95	Settled
2020-10-17 22:23:13 GMT+0300	194660003448	PUT	8319.71	8319.39	1.00	-1.00	Settled

Account	No. of runs	Total stake	Total payout	Win	Loss	Total profit/loss	Balance
VRTC3063965	63	63.00	94.35	33	30	31.35	46.35 USD

We continued to trade with this bot, broker gave us a winning series to keep us in trading, but at final we lost the money by 6 steps of martingale, The broker reached his goal and took our money, and after 78 runs

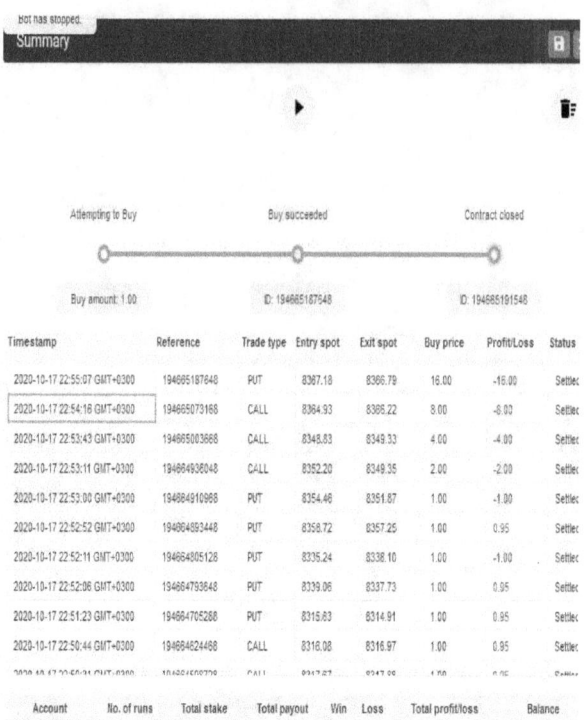

This is the ideal example of how this algorithm can work (it may be different in different situations, but the point is still the same in all bots trading)

WITH EVERY NEW SERIES OF CONSISTENT LOSSES IN ONE ROW, BROKER TEST YOUR DEPOSIT!

IF YOU RECOVER 2 CONSISTENTLY LOSS (UNSUCCESSFULLY TEST FOR BROKER) – IT WILL BE 3 LOSS IN ONE ROW

IF YOU RECOVER 3 CONSISTENTLY LOSS
(UNSUCCESSFULLY TEST FOR BROKER) –
IT WILL BE 4 LOSS IN ONE ROW
IF YOU RECOVER 4 CONSISTENTLY LOSS
(UNSUCCESSFULLY TEST FOR BROKER) –
IT WILL BE 5 LOSS IN ONE ROW
IF YOU RECOVER 5 CONSISTENT LOSSES
(UNSUCCESSFULLY TEST FOR BROKER)
– IT WILL BE 6 LOSSES IN ONE ROW YOU
CAN'T RECOVER 6 LOSSES AND LOSE
YOUR MONEY – SUCCESS FOR BROKER

We are sure that you will never see the bot that
starts to trade immediately catch 5-7 consistently
lose in a row after 10 – 20 runs (We have never
seen those bots too)

This is the manipulative method by which the
broker lures all new traders to trade on his
platform by using the bots. Such trading is
guaranteed to bring profit to the broker (loss your
money).

And so before further training, you need to choose one of three ways now*

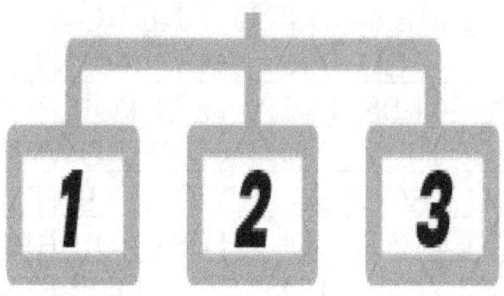

	Standard Version	
Standard Version **+ BPL STRATEGY** AUTOMATIC **and improving** **trading accuracy**	**Standard Version** FULL AUTOMATIC FULL	
		learning our method
0.35$ start stake **without martingale**	0.35$ start stake 2-5 stakes	
profit	40$ daily profit	20$ daily
80$ balance required recommended	150$ balance required 50$ balance	
the acceptable	Long run	

Long run acceptable
version for lower balance**

Most likely you will choose 1 or 2 methods and
we understand this, but we also hope that you
will be interested in how to get the most out of
this bot with the best results and minimal losses
with our guide.

<u>We recommend that you remember these 3 ways,
you will still need them to study the book</u>
- *We need to understand that trading on
  synthetic indices (artificial broker
  markets) we need $ 50- $ 150 to survive.
  The profit may vary depending on market
  conditions*
  All versions are attached to the package
- *You can start with this version if you are
  not sure that you can use our strategy*

DISCLAIMER

*Binary Options trading carries a lot of
risk to your capital. NEVER invest all*

your life savings, only invest what you can afford to lose. Remember, this is not Investment advice and the Binary Profit Lab is not in any way responsible for losses incurred. When investing in a Broker, read their terms and conditions before considering investing in Binary Option, in most cases do not accept their bonuses. Making money is a sure thing with this binary bot Venema PRO, but it can only work for you if everything is well understood and applied.

WE WISH YOU SUCCESS IN TRADING!

BINARY PROFIT LAB

www.ingramcontent.com/pod-product-compliance
Lightning Source LLC
Chambersburg PA
CBHW071952210526
45479CB00003B/903